HAVE YOU HEARD...
OUR CHILDREN
ARE HERE

Dr. Rebecca Dashiell-Mitchell

To order additional copies of this book, contact:
Xlibris
844-714-8691
www.Xlibris.com
Orders@Xlibris.com

ISBN: Softcover   979-8-3694-1678-5
       EBook   979-8-3694-1677-8

Print information available on the last page

Rev. date: 02/20/2024

A Special Appreciation for Family and Community of Friends!

Mother Rebecca, Nana Cornelia, Aunt Eugenia, Father Emmett,

Husband Lacey, Daughters Olivia, and Elan!

Our Children Are Here!
You promised to protect and show them the way.
Have you heard? Our children are here!

They will listen, ask questions, ask more questions
and learn! Our careful answers must inform,
show relevance and cause critical thinking!

Have you heard? Our children are here! They will smile more often than frown. They will challenge the known and the unknown and possibly turn this ole world upside down. They will respect our beliefs and values. What are our cultural sensitivities?

What are our values? How freely do you share your experiences and your beliefs? Have you heard? Our children are here!

Our children are here! They will lead and they will follow. They will live harmoniously with others.

They will appreciate the atmosphere, waterways, and the land. They will do these things because you have modeled and given a helping hand.

Our children will write and speak several languages. They will eat healthy foods to maintain a healthy body. They will create solutions for hunger, poverty, and disharmony.

Our children are here! Like you, they will deliver a positive message as they zoom across many lands.

Have you heard? Our children are here! You promised to protect and show them the way.

Just look... "We are all standing on the shoulders of giants."
Our children are standing on our shoulders peering into
the 21st century! One day soon, they will have global
intellect and shoulders strong enough to support others!

Whether at home or riding during family outings our children will ask questions. We must move forward with words and actions that will empower, communicate our collective high expectations, and strengthen our children's voices about personal values, familial relationships, and social issues. It is my belief that our love and our advocacy will nurture and empower generations of children borne and yet to be borne. Afterall, our children, our young she-roes and heroes, are society's passport to the future!

Our Children Are Here 04/01/11

Have you heard? Our children are here!
You promised to protect and show them the way. Have you heard?
Our children are here!
They will listen, ask questions, ask more questions,
and learn! Our careful answers must inform, show
relevance, and cause critical thinking.

Have you heard? Our children are here!
They will smile more often than frown. They will challenge
the known and the unknown and possibly turn this ole world
upside down. They will respect our beliefs and values. What
are our cultural sensitivities? What are our values? How
freely do you share your experiences and your beliefs?

Have you heard? Our children are here!
They will lead and they will follow. They
will live harmoniously with others.
They will appreciate the atmosphere, waterways, and the land.
They will do these things because you have
modeled and given a helping hand.
They will write and speak several languages. They will
eat healthy foods to maintain a healthy body. They will
create solutions for hunger, poverty, and disharmony.
Like you, they will deliver a positive message
as they zoom across many lands.

Have you heard? Our children are here!
You promised to protect and show them the way.
Have you heard? Our children are here!
Just look… "We are all standing on the shoulders of giants."
Our children are standing on our shoulders
peering into the 21st century!
One day soon, they will have the global intellect
and shoulders strong enough to support others!
Have you heard? Our children are here!

Dr. Rebecca Dashiell-Mitchell (Becca Dash),
"I Got My Breath Back" ©2011 .

About the Author - Dr. Rebecca Dashiell-Mitchell

Step into the enchanting world of Dr. Rebecca Dashiell-Mitchell, a spirited native of Boston, Massachusetts, whose heart beats with the rhythm of education and the magic of storytelling. For over four decades, Dr. Dashiell-Mitchell has been a guiding light for children and families, from the culturally rich streets of her birth town to the vibrant city of Atlanta, Georgia.

In her captivating journey as a Curriculum and Instruction Assistant Professor at Clark Atlanta University, she not only inspires the "critical eye, critical ear, and critical heart" of future teachers, she ventures into the realm of children's literature and digital storytelling. However, the true sparkle in her storytelling crown lies the fact that Dr. Dashiell-Mitchell is an educator; a published poet, "BECCA DASH," and Director of the Horizons Atlanta Clark Atlanta University Program. As one who loves teaching, learning, and exploring, she believes that words have the power to build bridges across cultures and generations. As a wife, mother, and Granberri she is most determined to make certain that children are empowered to become the hero/she-roe of their own story!

About the Illustrator – Mr. John A. Floyd, Jr.

Mr. John A. Floyd, Jr. was born in Fort Bragg, North Carolina and has traveled extensively as a child of military parents. His natural drawing ability was immediately noticed in kindergarten. From an early age and through-out his schooling several awards, medals, ribbons, and plaques were bestowed. Mr. Floyd was influenced by several master artists of diverse artistic mediums. Today, Mr. John A. Floyd., Jr., a renowned illustrator, specializes in portraits, sculptures, signs, and murals.

Printed in the United States
by Baker & Taylor Publisher Services